OUTLANDS & INLANDS

OUTLANDS
& INLANDS
Lindy Hough

TRUCK PRESS
St. Paul
1978

Acknowledgment is made to John Brandi (*Tooth of Time Review*), Ron Wray (*Primer*), Linda Parker (*Llama's Almanac*) and Michael Wiater (*Toothpick, Lisbon & the Orcas Islands*) in whose magazines some of these poems originally appeared.

Publication of this book was made possible in part by a grant from the National Endowment for the Arts, a Federal Agency.

Manufactured in the United States of America.
Distributed by Truck Distribution Service, St. Paul.

ISBN: 0-916562-15-8.

First Printing.
First Edition.
1978.

OUTLANDS & INLANDS

I. THE ALPHABET OF AGE

The Easy Life   /   11
The Apostolic Priest   /   12
Home Again: No. 34867   /   17
The Quiet Ones   /   18
The Alphabet of Age   /   19
People Are Separate   /   22
The Woman Who Thought of Herself as a Girl   /   23
A Plot of Ground   /   26
Morning Song   /   27
Leaving Maine   /   29

II. THE SPACES CREAK

The Poet's Metier   /   33
Keeping the Center   /   35
Wrong Number   /   36
Whale Singing Song   /   37
Vince Lombardi   /   39
The Ranks   /   40
Aware of One Another a Thousand Dogs Bark   /   41
Two Purgatory Cantos   /   42
To the Cape Elizabeth Ladies...   /   44
End of the Game   /   47
Stopping Living Coming Very Gently   /   48
The Process of Accretion   /   49
The Player   /   50

III. SHADOWS

The Hawkers   /   55
A Sunday Song   /   56
The Lesson   /   57
The Second Love Note   /   58

Altruism / 59

The Score and the Accompaniment / 61

Tensors / 63

Absence / 64

Dream of Night Before Rich Goes to Alaska / 65

The Absolute Seriousness of All the X's / 66

Tooth, Hand and Nail / 67

Out of Practice / 68

One More Time / 69

Human Form in Prison / 70

The Choreographer / 72

IV. ''CAN YOU PLAY TODAY?''

Leaving California / 77

Fragment / 80

The Stranger / 81

Family in the Desert / 82

Symptomologies / 83

No Time to Breathe / 86

Rt. 80 Out of Des Moines / 87

The Document / 88

The Betrayal of the Body / 90

The Miner's Daughter / 91

Shadow Play / 92

I. THE ALPHABET OF AGE

The Easy Life

There was a smoothie had a flat tire asked a studying law
student in a near-by apartment if he could use the phone
got the tire fixed asked the student if he'd like to
go for a drive to have a drink they do they drive into
the south of France visit relatives the law student has
liked since childhood
The smoothie shows him up the uncle becomes somehow
coarse and vulgar the neice who has always admired the
young law student sees how bumbling & awkward he is next
to the smoothie who flatters & charms her
on the way back after this long day after they stop
here and there for a few drinks the smoothie who is
driving too fast drives off a cliff escapes unharmed
the young law student is killed who had earlier that
morning been studying in the sunlight for his bar
exams
the smoothie tells the police sadly that he
doesn't even know his name, oddly enough
& it is sad because he too feels by this time very
close to the student
not to mention us the audience who by this time are
completely involved in the student's life nostalgia
memories self-confidence future mullings

The Apostolic Priest

Here is the apostolic priest
home on the apostolic range.

The Word
Travels.

Once the blessed is in
your head, all over
your body, like paths of ants marking you,
the sacredness of all simple acts,
roads, trees, dry dusty vacant lots,
does follow. Those paths are justly made.

I am assured of the succession
of the One
because the Word
does not leave.
It is intertwined
in my mind:
        you are one
        of a procession, mad & hungry,
        hunting down the spiderwebs
        arch themselves
        between my halls.

        Hark, says the portico.
        Quiet, say the pillars
            On top, says the sleepy masking
            sun,
                throwing its face beneath the
                contempt of the window panes.

        Proceed with danger, they all say
           in unison, because they know
           the taste of dry venison
           & unkempt beds.

        *   *   *   *

This is a bare house,
filled with a man's personal possessions.
Because a woman isn't living here presently,
      his things are all around, leap out
      at me & signify unusualness. It is
      unusual for a man to live alone. & what
      is unusual, if it does not fit into a stereotype
      but rather informs of a life, is
      attractive.

I have three beers (bears).
A headache lives here also.
It's hard to sit in this chair,
    because there's only a board
    across the edges of it which the
    cushion covers. It gets awry &
    he comes over to fix it while I stand.

I pet the dog
    because there's no other transformation
    possible.
I know the dog's not relevant, as I slide
    into talk about pets, but what is
    clouds and fogs my brain, is too inside,
    there are only blank windows.

I can't see outside.
This is the confusion of sexual attraction,
      named as stalwartly as others
         name war the most important activity
      of our days, *the war.*
Do I ring with shame that I'm not
      possessed with the talking of it,
      but am possessed of your presence
      instead?

(Many men somewhere
 did not attend to their immediate
 lives.

Many men somewhere
did make a war, did kill others
without need, did not tend their
particular bodies and gardens and homes.

Many men somewhere caused others to die.)

& this then is the *coming after*, not
  that you protest the war in all the public
  ways that you can, but that you
  tend your own house, not in a fire of
  isolationism, but with belief that if
  men did, they wouldn't start wars, or
  need wars to preserve what they've amassed.

This man
(those)
that I feel
a rush of wings
toward,
& those
that I live with,
   these do I count
   like the angels walking round
   the perimeter of my bedstead,
   these, wings of eiderdown,
   do inform my slightest touch.

   Quiet, brown,
   hair in the air,
   a figure in
   the doorway,
   thinking,
   speaking,
   unspeakably down
   & trembling,
   human figure,
   figure that files past me,
   that I can know
   & touch,

this if I care for,
can preserve
a world.

*   *   *   *

Who's this
coming along
the path
at this moment,

blown quite wild-frenzied
by some internal wind
ravages behind his eye,

what pistol's
held up to his throbbing temple
I can catch glints of, like a
shiny bit of metal on a field catches
the sun, a lake seen from a plane
catches, a minute, then is flat & matte —

he's lighting an endless pipe,
trembling hands, stockpile of
wood or patience or endless gestures,

these movements do inform
a man. They do speak for him.
How little he says.
How afraid he is of speaking.
(how I think I am loving him)

what archetypal image
is he dancing in my brain,
to so dictate with such serenity
to my sensibilities,

not, surely, showing his self to
me but some muse-like endeavor,
his dance, his surliness,
his down-and-outedness are all
a part of it —

15 /

my conscious mind knows too well
how to pick through green pepper tangles
        to come up with him.
He's not representing himself
at this party,
but some down-road nether wind
which he's blown the sands of
onto fifty million archaic fieldstone
years of grazing pasture,
as the land has changed
peoples, hands, animals,
still the wind blows,
still it is as specific as your name,
still so unfamiliar
I can't remember it easily,
generalized as the vagaries of
some tree-wrapped Kali.

Home Again: No. 34867

Delight (though there is absolutely
Nothing
To look forward to)
To come home

> Because we can't get a start
> Anywhere but here.
> As snows stop and wind says
> *Okay. Enough for this far north country*
> And goes off to Greenland,
To blow someone else's brain to bits,

> We rest,
> To become cotyledon.
> We can only move forward
> By the year nudging us there,
> Us, we would squat in the same old corner
> Mourn old shoes,
> Lost songs;
> Peripatetic visionaries
> Who move because the months nose us on.
> Still, March is ending.
> Still, it takes April to make
> Spring viable, grab as ice did,
> Last, for sap to drip

> Only when the weather turns
> Do we allow ourselves the calm to say,
> With coffee on the porch in the sun,
> We might be happy together.

The Quiet Ones

Speak
To the trees.
They know you better.
They're not going to
Let on; the silence,
The non-activity of spangled tears
Isn't what they see.

They've got it together:
A wind, a light snow,
A swamp beneath them that never dries up
When everything else
Needs to be watered

They are climbing towards
That launching pad
High in the sky,
They don't think
Of constantly starting over again.
They have patience, the slow burn of
Augustus, to wait it out.

Blue daisies in the field
Consider them friends.
They don't
Constantly have to stop
To tie a shoelace.

The Alphabet of Age

for Robert Creeley

i.

You want to date the poem,
  not by month, day, year,
but by the age: this was written by
a very young one,
this was written when a surge &
a life were in conflict, when an ease
was missing, when the breeze
immediately had to do with gardening
& seeds, and pulls circled the house
from the poem to the garden to the child,
& there were naps & meals & fucking
in between.

ii.

Life at forty
and life at twenty-seven,
and fucking for each,
so different. The tunes of
each, the resonances, the meaning
& the postures of each,
so different, different as two
species, but the same, for each
the renewing in the learning of the other's
world, cycles, day-spaces.

Twenty-seven is
mad with her immediacy,
is playing a tricky dead-serous game that almost
seems to threaten extinction,
weaving in & out of children & art & motherhood
& the rejection of all that & every role;

every question is serious,
only rarely does she flash with
the glint of the bliss-moment of beginning-
life & ending-life & fucking,
but often enough for life to come before death,
for the demand of that bliss to have life.

She has to yell loudly to summon irony,
who for forty and his friend is a
lazy drinking buddy. For her he lounges unconcernedly
down by the corral, talking to horses & cattle
& waiting for five o'clock.

     iii.

To twenty-seven, it seems forty lives
in a rich ease of adventurous loam,
most numbers are run past again,
he is crystal blue with wandering & his
earnest searching is over. There are types,
rather than individuals to fathom; any
explanation will do. Actions are square &
firm: there is wondering, but irony comes quickly
& one sleeps late after a night of drinking.
Twenty-seven can't get to sleep,
forty gets stoned if in doubt;
twenty-seven has to consciously fight the pull
to melodrama & sifts with an azure net all
statements for their intent, implications
on her possibilities.
Forty is a long way from being uppermost
in his mind, so familiar is he with the world,
but twenty-seven catches in him an easy obtuseness
towards girls and sex: difference rather than
understanding informs woman to him, she is a
separate species, always mysterious, a loon
poised drinking at a lake who quickly becomes magical.

The man of forty savours his family,
rather than seeing them as a restraining order,
he watches his friends' patterns in relationship:
this one talks endlessly of children
but has none;
this one has lost a closeness of talk &
    sensibility by a new life;
this one takes the concerns of the young
into the lap as the young do, and creates
a giant family of a generation.
& through all this sight
his place is clear, his ranch stays
in one place, he can travel
without being on the road,
he can entertain irony lavishly,
fertile in recollection & playfulness.

    iv.

Cotyledon &
full growth
meet and feel attracted
by the pull of age spanning a bridge
as much as genes or roses
in a windy world.
Twenty-seven watches forty, sees
a confusing but inwardly calm whirlwind,
to forty twenty-seven is another woman
and another man's wife
stitched in red along the surface of a rich fabric.

People Are Separate

He was who he was and I and a stream ran through the two. Who anyone cared, did anyone and if they cared did it so much as make a cosmic ripple, did he notice it or she anyway. Well both did in times of need it was necessary to know the property line, to know who owned what and which was his which mine which mine that he wished were his. No one quite really did know and both had been feigning not to care, as though that was too gross too outright but still there had to come a time when the house would be sold & then where to tell the buyers this is your property but I don't know quite how far it goes. So training his mind carefully on himself the details of only his present life and not the life he might lead in the future, he needed to decide where he stood.

While he was standing there his son got in the snowmobile and it proved exceedingly embarrassing. They were going to discuss the property line. As she was crossing her property to get to his property the small son lost control and the snowmobile plunged across her property and would have crashed into her house if the son had not luckily gotten control of it and swerved it back. That was unfortunate.

There were a number of harsh words about noise and property and the quiet white snow while it couldn't muffle the noise did cover the property lines, which no more existed than the equator did, a shiny tinfoil string around the big belly of the earth.

But still he did not know where the property line was. They stopped using their snowmobile at home and the son was considered secretly more defective than ever. The property line seemed to be there even more strongly demarcating as there were never any words between them, just a huge flaming wall of silence so there was no need to find the stakes and mark it out.

The Woman Who Thought Of Herself As A Girl

Take I

She was limited, but not alone because of her children. She had been
limited as a child, a teen-ager, a young lady. Now she was limited as a
stunted woman, roped into a cycle of too much Thorazine and in and out
of Maine State Hospital, but still, as she said to everyone, she was
not yet a freak.

She dwelt in the house of ordinariness. Her house was as difficult to
live in as the hospital, it was clear; the one was respite from the other,
but each had its own craziness. Never had there been piping in the
sounds of a world of richness and calm, but only incessant demand.
Before the children, it was the demand to produce the children. When
they were babies, it was all right; there were enough images in her head
about babies to make that condition tolerable. But as they grew older,
their specific selves took on form and their needs nudged into demands.
She could see the hydra-head she had produced getting out of hand. She
felt like a creek that had run dry. As she lifted one heavy foot before the
other, little eddys of sand tumbled down into her empty footprints.

She guessed she had not brought the separate things in her life
together sufficiently tight to form a mesh. She felt herself drifting out
through the large loopholes in her life's existence as the television blared.
When she chatted with a neighbor, the sameness of life she had always
known waved into focus and reassured her, but even as she retreated into
the house she heard the dull roar preceeding the panic. She wondered
whether she would get to the kitchen table before it overtook her, and
what the kitchen table would look like then.

When Melinda watched her take her slow walk each day, sometimes
she went to the road and walked with her, just for company. She listened
to her talk, and to Melinda the talk was much the same as the other
neighbor women's, except nicer, more friendly and less catty. It seemed
for them the world resided in units of sameness. The same material was
gone over again and again: the town, what to buy, what cost a lot now,
what one had bought at the Giant Discount Store. When the husbands
went to Guards for the weekend the weekend blended into the week-
days. People were pretty much the same except that some were rowdier,
some more shiftless and therefore had less means, some were different

and were outside. There was not much to learn, rather a right way to do things (having to do with neatness and orderliness) and a wrong way.

The woman who thought of herself as a girl knew that the neighbors thought she was crazy. She was embarrassed about the hospital, that she had to go there. But her house was as neat as anyone's, wasn't it? And she certainly stayed home. She didn't run around, as some of them did. No matter what happened, she would stay home, as long as her children needed her.

The Woman Who Thought Of Herself As A Girl

Take II

Green leaves are proper. Not brown leaves, which must be burned; black leaves are dirty. Deep loam, compost, bacteria, are all dirt, and therefore dirty. You must wash your hands. You will probably get infected. The green quatrain will fill up. Retarded, the loops the turtle can swim through are quite big! He can get out. But no knowledge grows on the sides of his aquarium because there is no space, money, joy, just sameness and an artificial light-bulb.

Some fish are rowdy and some poor. Some don't watch out for themselves or try. What can you do with a man just won't try. Or a fish, for that matter. Because we keep everything so clean, we look to have more money than we do. & because we don't look the least bit different (see how our jade lawn reflects our lovely eyes! see how our clean white driveway shows what soft white arms we have!) we look the same as everyone, we won't be singled out, no you could never say we weren't *all right* in the total eyes of collective america. Everyone is looking at us all the time.

A Plot of Ground

Leave me there
Wherein I came.
In sleep.

Carrying the child
Up to bed, quietly
So calmly he finally
Sleeps, how deep
Is the nape
Of his neck I kiss,
And want
Nowhere but here, ever
To go nowhere that isn't
Precisely in the best
Interests of this nape,
This nodule we made,
You and I in the best of our
Virgin-territory, hoeing
Working, trying very hard,
Because we have strained to farm
This good patch of marriage. Shouts go up
That therein on good soil the cherub stands.

Morning Song

Well I think you reach a point where you say
well the window is open a little if I opened
it more I could get even more air
& that is how it is with having children,
you can only do so much at one time,
you figure it is going to take twenty years
of your attention & by then you'll be forty-seven,
that's almost fifty and most of my life is over
then, so perhaps it is best to have a choice
& to just say well, I knew quite a bit of what
that world was like & I did not know quite
a bit of what the rest of the world was like,
& it seemed so easy to learn, & in truth
more interesting and as though I did have
the means to learn, that is had writing as a
way to travel lightly & when I wanted, very
heavily, getting quite deeply involved in things
& people, so I just said one Saturday the 11th of
December in 1971 after we had one who was two
and a half, that is Robin was just coming into
the month when his winter equinox would assert
itself, we just said perhaps it won't be so bad
for him alone, not always having another to refer
himself to to mirror himself in & although he will
lack a certain cozy companionship especially when
he goes to bed (remembering that American image
of the two children speaking softly to one another over
their soft dark covers) perhaps our world could
be really alive & constantly changing, not for
a minute getting trapped in housewifery and
limited family squabbles & this is what I thought
& was thinking about as I went about cleaning
up the diapers the toys the dishes in the kitchen
sink that December day when most of the population
was worrying about Christmas shopping & far away

Tibetan yogis were meditating about how to turn
their spermic energy back into their metaphysical
systems

Leaving Maine

Harpswell, Maine.
She plays the harp well.
That's all anyone remembered:
not how many flowers did she kiss,
not how many dishes did she wash,
not how many pins did she employ.

We are about to leave,
& they say, how we'll miss you.
Like people everywhere,
when we were here
we were not so accessible as
we seem to be going away.

Actually, we are no more a commodity
to be heeded now, either;
just that they disguise their envy
at movement and variety
(a new state! a new house!
a new job! new possibilities!)
in a flutter of wings beating
& loud cackles, like a chicken
who talks a lot when its head
is about to be severed.

II. THE SPACES CREAK

The Poet's Metier

What is my —
what you call it
my —
what can be described,
as, this poet
does this,
& that, this.

I'm a cat on a fence.
The fire horn blows.
Those who live around here
can tell where the fire is from listening.
Just like I'm not here,
geographically, never really
settled in here—
There's a skittering between my eyelids,
a sort of imbalance
only righted by walking
very carefully along the fence,
& then down another,
and another.

I cover whole cities that way,
fence by fence,
never touching wooden backporches,
never having to cross backyards,
so light in my cat step
I leave no tracks.

But I never know
where the fire is,
& my poetry to others
& my self
is not easily classified.

Is that a fatal weakness?
Does it mean that its
        not really *on*,

like it freaks me
but no one else?

If I wear a long magenta skirt
& a complex necklace
& high button black boots
& push my long brown hair behind my ears
with a quick flick of my hand so my face
can be seen better,
will I put it over -
& no one will notice?

Instead of spending $48 on groceries,
could I buy myself
some really far out clothes?
I'd rather be a cat,
walking successive winding fences,
silent
& moonstruck.

Keeping The Center

I go to bed in guilelessness,
wearing it artfully
as my new nightgown.
What a creation.
What a two-penny splendour.

I can't be anyone else
        but me.
Me down by the roadside,
me swimming up to the beach like
        an oil-slicked shark,
me bobbing out to sea like an old bottle.

Everyone else that tries
        to be me, that I
try to be,
comes to a bad end,
like a guided missile
that ultimately has to fall
        in the sea.
But words, stars, guilelessness,
emptiness is better
than being the one
who comes to tea.

Wrong Number

Perhaps one should depend on
immediate resources.

He is my *close friend*.
I can reach for him
he can give a hand
in the fawn-colored moments
when dawn is about to break
when one is exhausted from the evil hours
pitching bodies from the tower.

But he wasn't there
when I needed him.
So I called someone else, far away,
taking that chance.
I invoked a spiritus meant
for a different quest,
meant for forests & fern books,
for crises of knowledge,
not survival.
I confused my worlds, which always seemed
to be licking at one another.

No businessman would make such a mistake.

I took you for a dancing sailor
on a red sea.

Whale Singing Song

She is doing something
She is doing something
She is doing something

and nothing.

Sitting there looking out
Bypassing the window
her eyes see ships.

The ships are out
too far to see,
gliding the deep

The whales spout.
Someone on board sees this.
He who sees thinks of her
    at the exact instant,
    & she feels herself on board,
    seeing the split-second spout,
    there is a thrill there
    & she will tell the others tonight,
    when she gets home, undressing
        before the warm fire in the kitchen,
        her nightgown...

But she is already at home.
She is sitting at the window.
She is doing nothing
But thinking all this.

Hearing the songs of the whales.
Giant sperm blue-backed black
    killer whales!
        They play &, eventually, mate.
Searching for a cetology
    her mind is doing much
    sitting by the window.

Watching the non-existant ships
      unsailing,
Where she is in relation to the whales,
      Watching no spouting, feeling no
      thoughts on her back, her front,

She is doing something
She is doing something

Sitting by the window
Looking out
She is doing nothing.

Vince Lombardi

After the grand fight
After the grand fight
They went home at night

Wrestling football
they stubbed their considerable toes
    & had lost track
whether they hurt
    or not
It was not
    that the game was important
but that it was
    the only important thing.

So massacres happened
& men cleared the board
   to begin again.
Tried not to feel hurt,
Tried not to feel angry

After the grand fight
After the grand fight
They went home
      at night.

The Ranks

There was a moment in which slices of
Lemon were inserted into time
By a giant with peanut butter hands.

Everyone went home because the smell
& the taste of the lemon were too strong.

I defected from the first-grade walk
to the park when it went right by my house,
unable to be so close to its warm cocoon
of freedom and yellow desire & yet
still have to keep rank, file by, think
in the school's mentality of *going on by*.

Five times I broke, on five successive walks.
Coming so close to home & yet not being allowed
to go in was like a code in my mind,
dot dot dash. Let my life's internal noises make
some sense out here. Dot dot dash.
Let the outside & the inside become friendly.
Dot dot dash. Let more than moods
& imposed rituals from outside determine
what we do.

Aware Of One Another A Thousand Dogs Bark

Nothing that comes or goes is free. Is home free. Tastes like chunks of
black coal in the mouth, a horrible taste, coffee warmed up too many
times in your mouth, the taste of a good thing gone bad.

He and she and perhaps all of them all in the human race although they
did not say it, did not dine it in their daily bread or ask it to tea, were
attracted to people under their thumb. Who could not get the best of
them: the others stuck up like rocks in the path of roaring water, to be
gotten around, to be mowed down or smashed over somehow, perhaps
only in the fury and force of the pounding. As she watched it she could
not help participating, simply having been born and some mother
having put hours of time into making a viable position for her in the
world meant that she was out there with the rest, struggling and biting
and sighting the horizon for those that would block her progress and
those that would help it.

Who could not get the best of one. Who could not best one. Love and
war, competition, the daily market, IBM, it is up. It is down. Someone
loses from another winning. And finding those that you like, those with
whom on some equal footing you rest, a bank or a hill together a
semblance of definitions in common between you two.

The birds sang, singing in their way, concerned with their business,
whatever it was. Not making an effort or not having the ability to
understand or even care about human competition. Which did not work
the other way around, humans did feel responsible for understanding
bird-paths. & yet they were singing wholes, not parts, serene and frantic
in their arts, unconnected, unconcerned with human competition. Which
tried its best to subvert itself, counter to this trend ran a humanizing
loving trend, six individuals living together in an Ann Arbor town house,
really trying to lose images and love each other enough to make
something beautiful. Although we hear about it only, never travel to
Jerusalem to see it for ourselves, does it work, this is the Crusade. We
want it to work. We want to spend our time, lose our competiveness,
make some money, sell our house. We want to be born.

Two Purgatory Cantos

I. THE NEEDLE'S EYE

> ''we were climbing on
> a cleft rock which was moving on
> one side and the other, like to the wave which
> receeds and approaches''
>
> *Purgatory, Canto X*

The question is
the pass perilous:
a moving barrier, dirt which
follows the feet as they move in
the dust   so tiny the passage, it's
like a needle's eye, swaying in an
uncertain breeze propped up by a
collection of random boulders, random
thoughts of a giant mind who has perhaps
lost us, the needle, the path run through
like a thread, among his possessions in
disarray —

> either all is the same to you,
> the same faces in Denver & Cambridge,
> or the Way is fraught with difficult
> terrain

& even the sky sways
riding up it, one
looks for balance &
footing.

II. A BAD END

HUMBERT

;

the aristocrat.

my boots. ⎫
           ⎬   figure large in my
my cape. ⎭   *mappe monde*
they speak louder than the raven
of what i want, my place in society!
Beguiled by the puffiness of arrogance,
ancient blood, chauvinism of line,
Humbert is weighted down now
in Purgatory, by the stones of common
Humility
               as when new risen bread
               is brushed with accidental finger-
               tips before the oven,
                  & quickly
                      sinks,
               centuries of Risen-ness to a
               flat stone in
               5 seconds

To The Cape Elizabeth Ladies
Meeting At The Public Library
Reading: *From The Folks*
Who Brought You Pearl Harbor
To One Another

Daytime doldrums.
Knitting.
    Making loops.
Making daily sense.
     or non-sense.
Loose freedom of bodily activity,
   missing here. Rigid in chairs.
Not to move, the object here, as in school.
This book club is like the first years of school,
   show & tell, where you don't have to be
   responsible or really *know* anything
you just tune in & listen, if you dig,
& loose your mind if you
don't

Rob plays freely, lining up trucks & cars
on the lower shelves. Michael huddles in the corner
with his blanket, daunted by the stern glances from
his mother, who is herself uncomfortable.
I write freely.
We are tantalizing ourselves in this here book
(I swim into the collective of the group) by
reading about rich people. The book's concern
is advertising. It is an ad for advertising,
& we all are delighted. There is some attempt
in my mind to determine if this be the real rot,
the way men spend their time selling their products.
It is, but is far away

The Cape Elizabeth Town Ladies would bolt in fright
if a real rice crispie walked in, or a green giant
so here they are charmed, by someone young enough
to have been their son who has ''done well''

The money carries this book. Their interest in
it, the author's interest in it. The author and
they are justly worried about the kids under 25,
who, says the book, are going to ''take over'' the
world in a few years. They don't care about money,
which is why advertising is worried. The ladies
picture them as overrunning hoards (Huns) or Nazis
or messy mongrels, & discuss why they are so ''dirty.''

It's a very closed room. I become more objective
as the hour wears on, everyone knitting, those who
are not knitting with their eyes straight ahead on
the reader. No one has read the book, except the one
reading from it. They want to be read to, like the
children on the other side of the door who are read
to by Jaycee Wives.

My eyes continually meet those of
            a kindly grandmother one who smiles at me.
She is putting
            KINDNESS
                        out for me in
her smile like birdseed & I'm too much of a young
proud bigot to smile back.
I defect her glance
& think about how I look, properly dressed,
representing what they are suspicious of,
but camouflaged in their colors, not mine.

The ad man's words come out of the woman's mouth
as she reads. Words like *bread* for money, & we are
again slurping at the world of our children, the
swinging world he represents that we aren't in, being
too much in the box of our detergent. His language
cheapens everything. Death/war made cheaper.

War.death.Vietnam. War.Death. Vietnam. Killing.
There are bombs being dropped on peasants
mothers nursing/ peasants plowing/ peasants making lunch
as we sit here reading, being titillated by the advertising
world. Our country which is discussing advertising
& its glamourous overworked world at this meeting of
bored Cape Elizabeth matrons is dropping the bombs,
has made the harbor impassable.

WE ARE RESPONSIBLE.

                        *   *   *

    The ladies do not want to take responsibility.
They don't want to take the responsibility it takes
to read the fucking books every other week.
They want to be read to,
catered to,
protected by the government from Communists,
reassured they will get their Ban-lon
reassured it will be all right.

The country is too big
for them to have very much influence, too big
to understand. The complexity of the vastness
of systems daunts them, much as the workings of
nature & the real rise of the stock market
is beyond them. They've given up,
and needing to be entertained, don't want to hear
about the others somewhere dying.

As when I straighten up quickly after stooping, I see
purple on each plot of ground.
There might have been a chance here to live, but
they have lost it, buried in their smug humanity
& pettiness.

End of the Game

Sometimes the declarative falls away
language seems too heavy for sensibility
too many words in the world,
nothing need be explained.

All we want is to breathe air
walk in a new quiet place where
     no one knows us,
smell the rain,
realize the trees are so old, so patient
think about the vectors of older ones in
     the history of civilization, and
how they lived

Stopping Living Coming Very Gently

When you are stopping living in your life
The stars walking out of your eyes onto a long plain
When living is letting go and the strings are
      not tight enough any more
      the vectors missing
O Derrida that's it that's what I've been missing
O Foucault O yes what I'm missing is an annal of my self-hatreds

At those times you write yourself into the ground
you write about everyone but yourself
and cover yourself over with leaves, which freeze
you marvel how the first person, learned so faithfully, so well
is so sadly inappropriate to the big world

You launch into the second because maybe it has some familiarity
      without seeming so intimate
all your heroes are insubstantial
the real world fades away
you become a newspaper of the society's self-loathing
you spread bad feeling, apologize, but everyone's fallen asleep

The Process of Accretion

Poems build.
They have a life
because they're not trying to say anything
They're trying only to discover their own life.

They don't try to speak
   in any language but their own
They don't try to be declarative
or facile about anything

Poems are like clean rugs
and books about designs and patterns
Once you have felt a poem in you
    you're cleaner than you were before

Like a lot of artistry,
poems work best with a side winder
kind of focus, more akin to
prayer than comprehensiveness.

The Player

What happens is I guess coming down the road that his
car will not be there and when it is am amazed
because I have also ruled that if it's there I will see him
and entering the diningroom I don't but then do
and he smiles & says hi he is talking to some girl
a student perhaps
so now I am shaky and borrow money to pay for lunch and
sit down far on otherside of diningroom with someone else
and eat the lunch, carry on the conversation and leaving
I say hello Mr. Albright and he says coolly, looking me up
and down as I'm looking him also, how are you and I say,
pretty cool, in a tone that says I am holding fast to my
self and am not off-center though you give me no shift
and hurried he is passing on and me too outside

But it churns me and no longer am I good for anything
so go home and to him it is nothing,   it has always been
this way, this unsatisfactory
I put it together this way but still have the whole other
way to also spin out, that perhaps it churns him also and
he knows only how to handle it this way
But something in me a fear of authority   makes me
not able to cut through the webs of sticky mucuous in this
tangle and clear it out, like going up into an attic of
someone else's and seeing all kinds of gorgeous unusable things
and coming down and having nothing to show for that span of time,
say three hours
but the memory of such beauty

          Always this relationship has been this way and
still it has such power over me, in dreams and each time I see him
in reality, such a potency that there is nothing else more ''real''
in the life

          I wonder what fantastic grafting of spiritual-sexual issues
I have performed on this person who cannot grow into his role

who has no sensibility that would allow him to handle
his part, but who commands such dominion over his part that no
one else can hope to stumble along into it,
              because I have so carefully wrought it to his shape
his consistent unfullfilling actions that no one else could ever
have the tenacious combination of weakness and complexity to fit
into it

III. SHADOWS

The Hawkers

Shadows go by
Hawking visions.
They can't help it,
They've a product to sell,
A meeting-lane to keep.

They duck in & out
Of quick doorways.
They keep a fast-talking staccato
Time, as though sight
Were fervent & limitless & the change
Bouncing in their pockets
Could buy a real drink,
A real warmth made of wood
And flame, but I know in gingham & velvet
Shadows are only the damned, asleep.
Virgins are the buyers of visions without orgasm
And terrestrial saints are burned
After they have slept with angels.

A Sunday Song

Out of the daily
Out of the sacred day
Out of the rain blessing the day's fall
Out of the lilacs
bending to brush your lips with sweet
        water-drops,
Out of the highway from where we came
                to here,
Out of the book we have learned the Law
Out of our time we learned to use
        what was at hand & in us
Out of our cosmology we perceived
        the dance between us and its rhythms
Out of your mind I seem spun & wake
        in surprise to my separate existence.

The Lesson

I have freed myself from a destructive vision
and more and more
watch my core grow into its own turnings,
even as my fingers find the right chords
finally to play, I exult so much in the lesson
I lose my place and can't read the next note,

and play because exactly this exultation of
performance I haven't felt
in the work of the life,
but as though I were turning myself
inside out like a worn mitten,
taking out balls of fuzz
to fit a larger hand in,
so do I sense myself
cutting out suckers which sap my energy
and don't use it well,

excursions of thought
and fantasies based on others and
a view of others which is media-
based, an endless publicity stunt—

One lifts the pedal when the note is played,
and then depresses it, catches it again.
The counting now is not such an obsession,
the notes can be read, but with difficulty.
A tonic is the first note,
a dominant the fifth,
a sub-dominant the fourth.
It comes clear, like paste
when it has been well-mixed.

The Second Love Note

"A certain occupational type,
living under certain conditions,
upon a certain sum of money,
achieves a certain result in health."
            —Lura Beam, *A Maine Hamlet*

The apple blossoms I brought inside
to force
are blooming now, Rich

These crabbed branches
tossed then ripped off by the wind
in that rigid storm that tattered our
heads, to be iced the next day,
are blooming in a coffee can
I covered with blue burlap,
covered the bare table with a green tablecloth,
put them with spring drawings
      & a shell ashtray
beneath the mandala you made of the City
at night, our first and last lettered names
between a baseball and an arrow

I know spring, desire, hope
      gratitude, clarity
when I see it.
Through a long winter
we got,
and now it is so simple: fucking you
makes my headache go away.

Altruism

No one told me it was the fashion around here to go to the midnight church service so Robby and I drove in at 10 o'clock Christmas morning and went to church. For him it was the first time. We were lucky. There were hardly any people and no choir, just the organist and a few ministers and a few hardy single people but no other children. We sang hymns, I took communion, and Rob listened intently and didn't squirm much at all, but was happy when it was over. The minister quoted Lewis and Charles Williams and asked the question whether we didn't have courage to love other people given that Christ had so much courage. He wanted to know why it wasn't more obvious when Christ was born, given that God could have made it so, and why didn't God save Christ from his horrible death, given that he certainly could have?

"I want to know why!" he said, as though it were the question he had been carrying around with him all week, in much the same way I would have phrased my main question, I want to know why my body is cut off from feeling, and how I have gotten year by year more deeply into a dangerous physical-psychological situation. The minister answered that God probably did it all like this to make us work for the answer. He indicated that the same courage it takes us to take a chance on people and be hurt was the same courage it took Christ to do his deeds, even the deed of being born, without being bailed out. And the uneasy dualism of Christianity which has had me come last of all to myself as the object to focus on, after family, husband, children, was working right along in everything said in that church service: that to love yourself you must love others first.

I think that is not right. I don't believe it anymore. I think it takes a great deal more courage to take a chance on one's self and know one's self carefully, without hypocrisy, than it does to help other people. My grandmother was a Grey Lady, helping others in hospitals all her life, and now she is in a home for senile people and can't remember anything. What happens to people that they literally lose their minds, their bodies gone years before, so the details of people suddenly escape?

Here is a detail about you.

Here is another detail about you, and you.

But if they are not anchored to the core of myself, that core formlessly changing day by day and year by year growing into a complex molecular model, I will forget everything.

And as you have a family, and so many of your actions become for other people, it is hard to separate what you're doing for yourself and what for other people. But it's perhaps the central issue of being thirty-two, for me.

The Score And The Accompaniment

"Learning to beat the source of relation."
—*The Garden of Birth*, Edward Dorn

MOMMY MOMMY COME DOWN HERE
what is it robin
I need you to get another graham cracker
        yellow raisins for me.
You've had enough now.
What?
Me?
Enough?

mindless bumping of feet on the high chair.
One reaches adulthood to spend all their
time with children and the minds of children.

Children are left out of liberation talk
not because they aren't there but because they
must be subtracted to start with the premise
of an adult: a functioning human being (if the
damage hasn't been too severely done, if the
mind is not completely retarded or frozen in
fear, having hidden behind the skirts of children
as behind, earlier, the skirts of the mother)
able to decide what to do with a life. If you
add children, immediately the argument becomes
subverted and dominated: as in real life the
child can dominate over the functioning mind,
in an argument the needs and desires of children
are so insistent (the future of the race!!)
that they immediately become the *excuse* for the
retardation of adult happiness. A woman dominated
by children is an entirely different species
from a functioning adult. She is mad.

& yet
had I not this child here
who is playing now quietly safely & happily
would I even be home
would I have such an excuse
       to be here in the house
       writing on an April afternoon
could I create the remarkable tensions
out of another life
could I see yellow for yellow,
watch how language is learned by the human,
see what structures strike visually
& what is ignored,
catch what companionship is
         among one's own age-group
          & older ones & younger ones
flash on the remarkable perceptions
I did not teach
but which are being learned.

Learner, you are teaching me so much.

Tensors

I walk up the path to the dorm, filming. I am taking shots of my life, of my self as a representative woman, and doing a continuous shooting everywhere I go, retrospectively looking at my life, sometimes in satire, sometimes with bitter irony that it should have ended up this way, such a shambles of a life, sometimes with rich deep fulfillment that I have been so lucky. So rare! To have such a life, to have such opportunities that I can do just what I want, and only have to identify that.

The November air is sunny, crisp. The grasses are a deep green, no brown yet, it has not yet been so cold that the grasses have devolved into their protective brown.

I am too free, and it settles into a kind of loneliness, a use of solitude that I am only beginning to savour, to learn the richness of. The deep browns. The deep purple vistas of being alone. I think to cast myself onto a rock, like a piece of lichen—and move away when something is no longer comfortable. Just now I practiced, actually up for doing it; but after a while my attention wandered, I could take in no more and needed to feel a deeper connection to something, to someone, or to myself. I picture my book: the shape, the parts it is made up of, the salvaging job. I picture, who can I write a letter to—and then picturing the recipients at the other end, see them also wandering in a kind of haze, not much different than mine except perhaps more embroiled in a role from a job, reacting to, relating to that, instead of to a work.

The long definitions of a work: how the connotations change each day; how each day begins again an attempt to carry on what one is doing, to improve it, to shape it, to get it out in a form that is readable to others. To catch the Beautiful Thing! Sometimes I do it, and the work is pervasive as an orgasm, seems to be speaking in a voice fuller than my own being, to express the mystery that it did come out of me, but from where?

And that is why others around me explore very far back, to pre-Greek human endeavor, because they sense that it is not just now that makes up one's voice. It is also the voice of the Phoenecian fisherman, of Enkidu losing his tie to Gilgamesh, as that power-hungry king abandons friendship for dominion and loses humanity.

Absence

Sleep would nestle around my head,
it would be all right
except visions of icy paddles
hitting my head repeatedly
crawl into bed with me

There is no one there
to cuddle with, to bend my form round
to give the underlying additional heat
and my own warmth isn't enough—

So I am freezing. My chest begins to hollow out
No fire downstairs because I didn't make one
and you aren't here, so again I am caught up—
I have to make the house warm myself.

I get up to put knee socks on and 2 shirts and a sweater,
the night stretches,
with all its holes,
too thin, too long in
bone-brittle cold

Suddenly my smallest action is a worry.
Peace I had woven, albeit determinedly
from coffee & scrapbook & music & dancing children
has splintered into this jagged edge
once they sleep.
I wait for the cut into morning.

> Do you know
> > what a relief daylight is
> Do you know
> > what sunlight in the grey dawn
> > unexpected
> > can be to the sleeper who has huddled,
> > buried under blankets and
> > still shivering?

Dream of Night Before Rich Goes to Alaska

I'm living with another woman in a small town like Plainfield. I don't know any inhabitants but they know me. A man comes to the door, threatening me. I pick him up easily and tip him upsidedown, knock his head again and again against the steep stairs outside. Finally he's dead and can't hurt me anymore. I hadn't meant to kill him but at least it'll stop him from impinging on me.

I wander around the village with him in my arms, a crushed flat body. I can't figure out what to do with him—whether I'm ''guilty of murder'' so should try to ''dispose of the body'' or whether none of this applies to me and I'm free of these rules too. Maybe I can just go to the police—it seems that's what people used to do when encountering death on one's hands. They are on my path around the village square, so I toddle in.

(A couple is rehearsing ballet adagio in a house for sale across the street. Very attractive to me so I stop and watch for a minute). The police say he was already dead almost from taking too many cough drops, not to worry. They are nice, rather distracted, not very interested in my case but well-meaning. It's just not a very big deal to them. They're playing with their CB radios.

The character I killed was tall and dressed in a black suit, thin, young looking and drab. Not spirited—he didn't put up a fight. He's so out of it there's no good reason why he should want to live.

I awake thinking this is probably Peter, then that it's lust being killed matter-of-factly for spiritual gain. I feel somewhat relieved that all this didn't happen, but as I write this I know also that it did.

The Absolute Seriousness of All the X's

In the lunchroom she was uncomfortable because there were too many people who offended her, were in someway offensive. Mostly it was because she was ambitious but they seemed to have the jobs she wanted. They would not hire her. She was afraid of being thought a hanger-on to the college, a faculty wife, a lost woman, a madwoman, a parrot. She kept reading her book and wondered if anyone would sit down beside her. She fantasized that the man she was attracted to would see her, lonely and reading her book, and want to sit down. But when she looked up there were only the repulsive faces she didn't want to see. This really was being stranded in the midst of the forest but there were no trees, just pasty-brained people.

   She knew all this was snobby thinking but she kept on with it anyway because it was a friendly dialogue to have with herself and Martha Graham, whom she was reading about.

Tooth, Hand and Nail

She fought her husband. She thought he was to blame for everything. If she was able to pin it on him, then she wouldn't have herself to blame, and she could still be a North American Martyr. It was so peaceful being a martyr. They had wings, they committed suicide, they cried while others were uncomfortable in their dry eyes, they thought it would all end.

But it didn't. The next morning after throwing her horror scene she got up and looked in the mirror and was shocked to see her eyes were terribly swollen, simply from crying. No one had hit her. No one had told her what to read or where to go or where not to go. No one had kicked her out in the world, taken away her money, stolen her children, or deserted her. She had no one to blame but herself for her swollen eyes. She began blaming the footstool, which she must have run into the night before in the dark.

Out of Practice

She knew that she had to go practice because if she didnt't, she wouldn't be getting anything out of it. She had to have discipline. That's what makes the world go around. People in the dorm were smoking dope, and she could think of others who were hasseled by their children now, and she wasn't, so really she should use this spare time and go practice.

When she got to the piano she stared at it and it seemed to rise up on itself and bite her hand. It was a good excuse. Pianists always were hurting their hands and then they were not able to practice for a while. She intended to tell her teacher the next day that the piano had bitten her hand and that's why she couldn't practice. But she was out of practice at lying so she supposed she would simply be embarrassed again at not having learned the notes better.

One More Time

She kept inviting him over. She had to import his body into her livingroom always just one more time, to get a last glimpse. She kept wanting to have dinner with him, and so they did, but he was a curious mixture of passivity and aggression. She was beginning to understand that two things were possible: one, either he spent all his aggression on the college, where he fought giant campaigns with many soldiers and the most brutal and intricate of weaponry and had no aggression left for his personal life, or, two, he didn't like her and never thought to call *her*.

But, of course, what she really wanted, was to be called, adored, summoned. She wanted to be Helen to her Achilles, Cassandra to her Agamemnon. She thought of herself as the mysterious sign bearer, who knows things without having to be told, who walks around on the ramparts, watching the battle from above and dropping signs, signals, which only those most enlightened, like her Achilles, could see. But, of course, he *was* really fighting, whereas she was really not walking around on the ramparts, but home mending the children's things, where she should have been, or practicing the piano. He thought he was fighting for his life, because the college and his self had become One in a non-mystical transformation.

He was, of course, an existentialist. When she was cocky and lively he took it as being too strong, brittle, especially, bitchy. She had a whole life going, which filed quietly out the door whenever he appeared, so involved was she in him. And, in truth, she had always been this way, had erased any trace of her personality when men were around. But she was attracted, wasn't she, and so wasn't that worth it? What she dreaded was getting in a fight with him, and so she dreamed of mysterious .38's and .45's that showed up in hidden places, and that one day he would shoot her absolutely dead. It would be worth dying for, but what was it?

Human Form in Prison

Here is a poem that is a lovenote to
a world where madness and sanity sit
back to back on the shelf

of another's expectations of order.
I come in and the other
is always worried

about what I might do.
It's as though I have a knife
tucked into my shirt,

that I am too capable of hurt,
that I must blunt myself
because I am too strong,

too sharply piercing.
The other must be quite afraid.
The fact that my child

talks constantly of poisons now
probably isn't irrelevant.
Perhaps we are poisoning

one another, in trying to produce
domestic harmony.
If pleasure is a word we are too old for,

and meaning is only to be found in books,
that leaves me
with a knife in my belt,

waiting for a hole in the net
I might enlarge
to escape.

Everyone who comes
I pounce on as allies
in my attempt.

At the prison the guards are so lax
prisoners pile picnic tables
& climb over the walls.

The officials laugh nervously
and say there's no drug problem
in the institutions.

What do they talk about in their meetings?
They talk about poisoning one another,
but they talk in political terms

and mainly try to keep out
divisive elements.

Once you are a threat to one
penal institution
you are a threat
to them all.

The Choreographer

When you ''set'' a dance on a person that is magical
no other dancer can ever come along and dance it exactly
because all the movements, the curve of the arms and
fall of the weight were worked out with your first joy
at the movement trying to grasp onto that original dancer's
body and partly because of her or his body

That translation fits like a new glove and though someone
can travel from London to Stockholm to Stuttgart setting
Mr. Balanchine's dances no one can ever dance it like
Farrell or Kent or Kirkland, and the memory of those created roles
is like the original bronze casting, is indelible in the early
critic's memory who saw the part first with the original dancer

And is that not how the life goes
afterimages preceding us of the few experiences
we must have been created for, and they are really enough,
at the young age of thirty-two I think I've lived enough of the
really great ones to be only making further
permutations of actual occasions, draping them onto everyone
and everywhere I go whether each fits very well or not

So walking around in my life are shambles of ghosts, who
drape themselves rather baggily in their costumes, but I like
best the ones which seem to fit, and the ones which go all
the way home with me are those that glimmer like the original,
like the memory of a doll up in the attic I never brought down

IV. "CAN YOU PLAY TODAY?"

Leaving California

1.

when I get home
I want to cover all the pillows
with rich deep spider-cloth
and find all my lost kittens
tame them again

   conduct most meetings by candlelight
so our livingroom won't have such access
to the commonplace

I want to store up in my lungs
that good deep full rich air of Vermont
and watch the river carefully
and ride my bike over to your house
and teach you shiatsu
or maybe just do it on you
so you can see how unafraid of touching
I have become

2.

It will be interesting being in Vermont again
it'll be like ''Look, Ma, I'm flying!
See? I can live here too!
   Look ma, I can adapt anywhere,
I can live anywhere, in anyplace,
upon any planet, in any slime,
in anyone's boot, on anyone's island, on
anyone's lobsterback, look Ma, here I am again!''

But it will be so quiet.
I'm afraid of the moisture that'll
   get underneath my vertabrae
And no crazy people
And it so green, so sane
Nobody watching the hummingbirds

And what will I do in that calm
in that bleakness & how will I run from
    my kitchen when it begins rolling me up
in its linoleum floor

        3.

This is how it goes in my world

Wendell tells people about lobsterfishing
in the Oceanarium in Bar Harbor
but, he says, the thing doesn't flow right
and the man won't change the exhibit

Diane covers her notebooks with the most lovely
collages   they become precious magical lapis
she will put the postcards of various angels on them
she has just brought from Italy

Her rooms are like her notebooks
all the spaces are sacred
Her life becomes like that too, guarded
She controls it, utterly in a way few of us do

Paul comes down from Idaho to Berkeley
he speaks very quietly
I think how terrified all my family in Denver will be
when I am hardly speaking at all
Silence can be the ultimate weapon
What you do say suddenly becomes very important
when you say very little
And you have time to watch
Spiders speak very little
They wind their webs
When too big a catch gets in and pulls the whole
    thing down, they let the intruder lumber away
Then lug the strands back up to the starting point
and start all over again

Whenever the people in my world seem to shine
with a certain brilliance
my world seems ok again

    4.

what I miss in my father's
non-presence is
that connection to the dissolute

I have the fantasy he would
like my work and dig it for himself,
not place it at arm's length, to not be
discussed if one can help it
as the rest of my family does

it seems to create some awkwardness

My mother is mainly happy
when we discuss her lovelife
so I do that as much as possible

but underneath my feet is seeping a
cold dark black sewer
and I try to bang the head of the intruder
hard again and again
against the stone steps

and then I carry his body around in my
arms throughout the whole village,
asking,
what should I do with it?

    5.

I don't feel my father's presence.
I feel his absence.
I feel he's under the ground
and because he believed so little
himself/he is atomotized
into zillions of tiny little particles

Fragment

She didn't particularly trust him, and she *really* didn't trust herself with him. She had, as usual, known him too well in fantasy. They had experienced too much, in dreams, in the early morning waking hours when she pulled him up around her neck like a warm blanket, warding off the day. In life, she had no idea what he would do or what was proper or what he was thinking of when he looked blank at her, seeming to stare. Maybe he was blank. Looks which she took two weeks ago to mean some special connection to her, she realized now could just be a rather blank countenance on the world.

Her ideal was to be able to gather up the fullness of one's being and bring to another person all the richness one has seen in life, like a gift. She thought that her body probably showed exactly what she had been through in her life, and that even the act of talking with someone was an intimate thing, if one was really connected to this vehicle of multiple histories. She was approaching a new morality: that making love, then, was an ultimate generosity, a chance to tumble out this past non-verbal history like a dance. One would feel richly the pervasive gentleness flowing to all parts of the body, the legs and thighs and arms and groin warming in giving out and taking in all this from another person giving it all too. Such a gift was so sacred, so powerful that it could not be given very many times; the explosions which resulted emotionally from such an exchange were not for a person to know too many times. The intensity of being thus with another person was great enough that the rest of the time should be spent alone, in contact with one's self only, if only to process the reverberations from such exchanges and store up reserves.

As she met men who continually had no idea what she was talking about she began to see that they had different moralities. They were interested in conquest, and she was the prey. She began to feel hunted. Soon she took no chances, and didn't stray out alone.

The good clean snow. The patterns of snow in the crisp morning.

The Stranger

I notice that most of the world
is trying to water down
the language one has tried so hard
to uncover

It's the same process, the editors do,
the mothers do, the fathers I make my men into,
they want a little more class
a little more relation to the world at large
a little more plain-speaking

In therapy groups they are especially
suspicious of language
''too many words'' they say
and when I am about to cry,
''I hear tears''
as though it is a victory, see
we can undermine your sensibilities

What kind of radical vultures are these
reporters, these interviewers, these therapists?
These are my friends?
This is an economy I participate in?
These are people who would be my friends
only if I were to be like them,
only if I made myself consciously in their image,
scrawny and unsure and terrified of the world

I would have to be
a spider living underwater,
fueled by a shiny bubble
into which she drags her prey for safekeeping,
forgetting all the variable images of the world
she once knew

Family in the Desert

Look how easily he goes out the door.
He fairly glides, like a knife in water
or a man going through a mirror
to meet his Death.

He goes out the door easily
because I am here.
Mommy and Baby are at home,
where they should be,
stoking the fire, cleaning the floors,
taking care of each other.

Daddy likes to do the going-out.
He doesn't like Mommy to be out
and him home alone;
it's not cozy without Mommy there.
He *really*
doesn't like Mommy driving far,
or at night,
because she might trip
on a sense of herself that is strong
and can explore the world
and her Death
without Daddy.

Symptomologies

Violent reactions! at not being outdoors enough!
> I get up and walk outdoors and sit
> > in the backyard.

Violent reactions! at writing slick prose,
> > very tight, about dance I know nothing about.

Violent reactions! while being jealous of
> > Anne Waldman wondering why I don't have
> > her ambition or intellectual focus
> > or chutzpa or brashness or tolerance
> > for people.

Violent reactions!

Violent reactions at how hard, how much pure physical effort
> > it would take to get this garden into shape
> > when I am so lazy.

Violent reactions!
> > at not being loved ever enough at the right time

Violent reactions! of self-hatred at myself
> > being so bitchy to everyone

We need a rake!
We need a new trash barrel!
It's not worth it, we're here for such a short time?
We need to know why (to any number of people)
> > we can't fall into one another's arms
> > and make love easily!

My hair falls out, my arms fall off, my
legs crumple up, my fingernails slip off the
arms lying on the flagstone, my eyelashes drop out
one by one, my lips slide off to the side, my nose
caves in and falls in my lap, my ears suddenly seal,
my eyeballs leap out and float up into the sky
like a helium balloon, my breasts slip off my chest and
roll like tennis balls through the basketball hoop,
my cunt seals itself over like a lost cave, all
the hairs in my pubic hair become smooth and plastic-
coated.

       Violent reactions.

Always you are so complex and so accurate.
If you know the correct symptomology
there is a correct remedy. They add up into
a complex, and if you stop it now you won't get cancer.
Always you speak whole pages
     and I cry and am speechless, dominating the
     emotional floor, there is no more room for you.
     You envy that I can cry and I would wish to speak,
     but there are no words worth saying, and I can hold
     the floor and myself better by crying.

Well here we have come
all the way to California
where there are so many unemployed people
leaving our isolated rural existence behind,

and thank god

the tall brown-wood fence is high enough

that we can't see any of them

and they can't see me crying

Violent reactions! to all the events

       preceding my period, *always*,

       but I never remember.

Violent reactions! of disgust

       that life is so difficult,

       when I and we are so lucky,

       and all the credit should go

       to you, and you, and you and

No Time To Breathe

I've been away quite some time
from the northeast,
but I know when I get back it will seem
like no time—will we all have the grace
to pick up where we left off?

The trains of Berkeley go whistling thru
at about 9:30 p.m., the children finally asleep
and quiet moves in, lonely like the fog coming on us,
the brisk rustle of the night seabreeze,
a sax next door beginning
windows I must shut & lock in this downtrodden neighborhood

Listening earlier,
Robby & I think they come from the west,
but of course they're down by the bay, preparing
to begin again to cross the country,
their mournful whistles and clattering

Finish your story, I said,
when he couldn't think of any more to be said
A story should not be left unfinished
    Part of the work is to try and not leave
    our lives unfinished, but to reaffirm a totality,
    every day

Rt. 80 Out of Des Moines

What I want is for people
to not have to read it in a magazine
to understand themselves.

Imagine if people came up with
ideas about themselves on their own.

****

I want to deal
sapphire. Goods, hard stones.
Hard knocks. Difficulties that people
come to grips with/crying,
breathing deeply into their chests,
letting the ways they arrange themselves
fall away.

I'd like to deal in people who
don't place too much stock in
money, intelligence, or consciousness.
Even that.
Consciousness of consciousness can be killing.

Imagine pulling your shoulders back and
yelling, loud, really loud. I imagined
doing that to you all the way across
Highway 80 through Des Moines and Iowa.

The vision of the locked-up ones,
who chatter too much, who are too busy,
the herds of people while the crickets chirp
in Salt Lake. Even Salt Lake is nice of a summer's
eve.

If I had three wishes this morning they would be:
that Russia cease wanting to take over the world;
that people would push their stomachs out when
    they breathe;
and that people would stop trying to make more money
    than they need.

The Document

When the body is not what it is,
it shall be what it is not.
        Olson, *"In Adullum's Lair"*

A Scary Dream. October 5, 1976

I am scheduled to die by taking too many hallucinogenic drugs. It is a very gentle ceremony, arranged in the best of taste by loving and kind people. There's no reason why I'm to die, and I don't resist—it seems inevitable. My name is on that list—Hough, mispronounced. Others on another list will take 3 pills and won't die. Six others besides me are to take too many.

As the ceremony of the dying nears closer, we are given a paper with final instructions on how it will be. I'm to go to my room and put my head on a blue blotter after taking the pills and wait for my brains to seep out.

Getting the paper, I begin to realize that I don't at all want to die. Up to now I have mainly been terrified by the fear of dying, how uncomfortable the actual dying will be. Now I begin to think that others are going to be affected: my children are suddenly going to be minus a mother. I have a lot to do, a lot of life yet to live—there seems no good reason why I should die, no one has told me anything about things being better if I do, and I am curious. The paper in my hand seems to give me the beginning of a consciousness and a tool: I could show others this, perhaps they would think it bizarre and wrong. I begin to enlarge my perspective almost visibly, almost like a fly flying up from the bottom of a funnel vortex to the wider rim. There may be a higher authority than this, perhaps I have done nothing wrong and there is no reason why I have to die.

Beginning to question it, immediately I walk out and easily escape. I see that nothing is holding me back, that I can leave. I wake up amazed that none of this is true, that I simply lay in my bed dreaming it all and there is no possibility of really dying.

Death by disorientation. Benign people (everyone I've been associated with in Vermont) lead you to your death by their lack of perspective, their trammeledness, their limited and threatened assumptions in work and social life. Only by seeing the tribunal for the small affair it is, is it possible to escape it.

The Document: once I have something in writing that I can show someone else, they can see how warped the situation is. That I can show *myself*, because it is me realizing how bizarre this is from the document that awakens my consciousness that I might get out. Too bad to have to have it in writing, but there you are, we all have our limitations.

So the need to clarify the writing motive—I get mixed up when I think it is to show someone else (more hustling, more publishing)—it is only necessary for myself, to show myself growth and perspective—literally to keep myself from dying by not perceiving situations with enough perspective to get out of them before they kill me.

The Betrayal of the Body

"to passionately affirm and reaffirm..."
—Barbara Hepworth

The form of my father's life
was deviousness.

Since he could express no voice
or no feeling, he ringed himself
with tiny small pleasures,
which never grappled with the size
of a man's need.

He went to the PenCol Drugstore for a sundae.
Maddened, my mother burrowed down further
into martyrdom, losing herself as she slid.
She would need the world's richess.
She would need bubbles.
A stiff plank, extended out to her.
She would need to float.

She was just a woman, uncovered to herself,
weighted down in a world she felt powerless to change,
which she decided she wasn't a part of.

When I came along and declared the world
viable, affirmable and mine at thirty-two,
I staggered her and maddened her into torment
at the strength she had probably had, the years
of unliving she had worked so carefully,
tied in such precise knots.
She was too far along in a process of layering
herself over with paint. When I spoke
we watched in amazement at the years of terra cotta
and plaster of paris which cracked and tumbled
from her form. When she began to dance again
we marveled at the power of a body to sustain life.

The Miner's Daughter

The shape of my father was

caved-in.

The shape of his stomach was dead. If
the muscles were dead, the groin would not have
to feel anything, or miss feeling.

The shape of his body as totality was small,
caved-in, not a broad base from which
to expand, not dug into the ground because
really what could you do if one leg was shorter

Because he could not breathe from his stomach
his chest never developed, his neck sat
like a chunk of wood on a curved bowl
So there was no area, except perhaps his arms,
which took in or let out strength.

Tree base
fish base
rock base
basalt base
there is a rockbottom basalt base to what you're saying
We mine granite around here, not uranium,
I don't know about you.

We mine one of the hardest substances in the world.
Shined, it can eventually reflect you.
It is pretty expensive,
as are all the parts of our bodies.

Shadow Play

This is the way the world sounds:
        very quietly.
It moves along, just when you have it
        resolved into a structure,
there it goes again, moving off
My thoughts vibrate as they approach a higher note,
you can hear me debating
whether to fix a resolve or go on...
        and then dropping it, to let
what happens come out, like the sun.

The world, really,
is so quiet.
It is we who are the noisy ones,
who retch in our demands and judgments,
making ourselves unhappy, stirring up trouble.
We squeeze the night down into tiny orifices
we can't get through.
        The night isn't small.
        It opens vastly, it is the same landscape as
in day, only black. Because there is no light,
you should be able to perceive it better, use other senses,
not feel you are given ''less''.

I throw myself out of the bed,
down to the livingroom couch,
it seems more spacious.
It is the same night,
downstairs.
The quality is moe permeable, though,
        I feel I can move freely through it.
I turn out the light in Miranda's room,
        returning to bed after a long while,
and wonder if she will mind the dark.

She doesn't.
Slow trees, slow air, slow being.
      Let me be calmer, more sure,
      in my coming into being, this fall.

Lindy Hough was born in Denver, Colorado in 1944, and received a B.A. from Smith College in 1966. Since then she has taught writing and literature in various colleges, and has lived in Maine, Michigan and Vermont. She writes for numerous publications on dance and the performing arts, and presently lives in Oakland, California.

OUTLANDS & INLANDS
is published in a limited edition of 600 copies,
26 of which have been numbered and signed by the poet.

Typeset in twelve point Holland Seminar.
Designed by Mary MacArthur.
Cover photo by Joyce Tenneson Cohen.
Printed by Thomson-Shore, Inc. for Truck Press
in September 1978.